How to Build Super sales Funnel for Consistent Sales

Sales Funnel Marketing

[O. Addey]

Copyright © 2021 ***O. Addey***

All rights reserved.

Table of Contents

Introduction 6

Chapter-01: How to Build a Powerful Sales Funnel 7

What is a Sales Funnel? 7

Understand the 4 Sales Funnel Stages 9

Step 1: Awareness 10

Step 2: Interest 11

Step 3: Decision 12

Step 4: Action 13

Chapter-02: How to build Supersales funnel for consistent sales 15

Supersales funnel 15

Why are a sales funnel important? 16

The Sales Funnel Explained: How it Works 16

An Effective Sales Funnel Example 17

How to Build a Sales Funnel Fast 18

Step 1: Analyze Your Audience's Behavior 18

Step 2: Capture Your Audience's Attention 18

Step 3: Build a Landing Page 19

Step 4: Create an Email Drip Campaign 19

Step 5: Keep in Touch 19

Chapter-03: Measuring the Success of a Sales Funnel 20

  Why Should You Optimize Your Sales Funnel?...... 20

  How to Optimize Your Sales Funnel 21

  Have you ever wondered how businesses offer their products and services continuously?...................... 22

  Conversations in groups. 22

Chapter-04: Building a sales funnel from scratch..... 24

  KNOW YOUR AUDIENCE 24

  POSTING CONTENT ON ALL YOUR PLATFORMS .. 24

    BUILD A LANDING PAGE... 25

    LAUNCH AN EMAIL CAMPAIGN 25

    CONSISTENTLY REACH OUT 25

  WHY ARE A SALES FUNNEL IMPORTANT?............. 25

  Successful Sales Funnels Need Filling Constantly . 26

  Here are five tried-and-true methods for consistently filling your sales funnel 27

    Talking to strangers 27

    Network; don't sell 27

    Work on your elevator pitch.................................. 27

    Speak up 28

    Follow up 28

Be useful 28
Be an exhibitionist! 29
Chapter-05: Successful lead generation at an exhibition 30
Stand out and stand up! 30
Follow up (again) 30
Attractive content 31
Facebook Ads 31
Website lead magnets 31
Socially acceptable 32
Get them on your list 32
Build Twitter lists 32
Conclusion 33

Introduction

Each level of the sales funnel affects consumer behavior. You must be thoroughly acquainted with them. Knowing each stage allows you to employ techniques to increase the number of people who go from one step to another. This has the potential to have a significant impact on your business. Assume, for example, that you increase the number of people at two levels of your funnel. As a result, you more than double the number of leads and the percentage of closed clients. This implies you'll obtain four times the number of new clients every month. One of the most important business tactics is to define and manage your sales funnel. It takes time to create and optimize a sales funnel. It's difficult to work. However, in a competitive market, it is the only way to survive. Believe it or not, a seemingly little aspect such as font selection can impact conversions. And if you press them to buy from you too quickly, they will go. Take the time to build a sales funnel that represents your desires and the desires of your target audience. Cultivate it over time, change your approach at different phases of the sales funnel, and figure out why your efforts aren't succeeding.

Chapter-01: How to Build a Powerful Sales Funnel

As a business owner, you must promote your products and services carefully to increase sales conversions. This means that your marketing activities must be effective enough to generate leads for your company. Otherwise, your marketing investment will cause unneeded financial harm. As a result, intelligent internet marketing is essential! Building a strong sales funnel is one method to do this. You may already have the marketing materials, strategy, and money in place to publicize your company. However, you will not see any real benefits as a result of this. But don't worry; you did nothing wrong. You need to improve what you currently have to ensure that your marketing efforts result in genuine results.

Today, we'll look at how you'll be able to do so.

What is a Sales Funnel?

In essence, a sales funnel the series of stages or phases that a consumer goes through to purchase a product or service. This approach guarantees that your marketing efforts result in conversions.

As we all know, not everyone who sees your marketing materials becomes a buyer. However, you may plan your marketing operations to keep an audience interested. They are well on their way to becoming a customer if you capture their attention correctly! The notion of a sales funnel might vary based on how granular you want to maximize your efforts. However, the sales funnel design indicates four critical phases to converting an audience into a committed customer.

One of the essential ideas in sales and marketing is the sales funnel. The narrow bottom of the funnel represents how many of those leads are converted to customers after the sales process. In contrast, the narrow top represents the aim of any firm – to produce as many leads as possible. Sales funnels are all around you, even if you don't recognize them. For example, a client comes into a large department store and notices a rack of discount shoes. They move closer to the rack, look at a few prospects, and fit a couple of pairs - they've progressed to the next stage of the funnel. The consumer then chooses one pair they can't live without and walks to the counter to pay. They've arrived at the final stage. If everything goes as planned, they complete the transaction and reach the bottom of the funnel.

The sales funnel represents each step that a potential client must take to become a customer of yours. Let's take a look at a standard sales funnel. People at the top of the sales funnel to pass through your business. A certain number of them opt to walk in; this is the funnel's next step. Next, a client notices a rack of discount T-shirts. The thumb through the rack, and they've progressed to the next stage of the funnel. The buyer then chooses four t-shirts and proceeds to the checkout. They've arrived at the final stage. If everything goes as planned, they complete the transaction and reach the bottom of the funnel. This process occurs in some form or another in every firm.

Your sales can include any marketing channel. Furthermore, your funnel may be dispersed throughout many channels.

Here are some things you should know and plan for before establishing a sales funnel.

1. **Brand**: You must already have a well-established brand and business scope. You can't sell something that doesn't exist. By correctly building your brand, you will generate a message that you can run with.
2. **Problem and Solution:** The primary reason individuals buy commodities is to address a problem. Your message must address these issues in some way. Furthermore, your message might mention how your product can enhance the lives of your target audience.
3. **Audience:** In digital marketing, targeting is critical. There are tools available to assist you in tailoring your campaigns based on your target demographic. So you're ready to begin after you've identified your target audience!

Now, let's get into the specifics of the sales funnel. The four steps of the sales funnel idea are as follows:

Understand the 4 Sales Funnel Stages

The four steps of the sales funnel are easily remembered by the abbreviation AIDA: Awareness, Interest, Decision, and Action. These four stages describe the attitude of your prospective consumer. Because you don't want to deliver the incorrect message at the wrong moment, each step necessitates a different strategy from you, the marketer. It's like a waiter asking you what you want for dessert before you've ordered your beverages and appetizers. So, let's go through each stage of the sales funnel in further detail.

Step 1: Awareness

During the awareness stage, you aim to reach out to as many individuals as possible and inform them of your existence. Ask yourself, "What can I do to raise awareness of my company?" This is the point at which you initially capture a consumer's attention, most likely through advertisements, content marketing, video, or a social media post. In a perfect world, customers would buy right immediately. Unfortunately, it is not how life typically works. This phase seeks to increase the visibility of your company. While you may have already established a niche or demographic, it is OK to broaden your marketing efforts to include similar groups. For example, if you offer high-quality gaming accessories to professionals, you may also choose to reach out to beginners. Your product's ability to improve their gaming experience might be your selling point. The essential thing is that you made your brand prominent and stated clearly what issues you intend to address. This is also the stage at which you actively advertise your brand rather than your product. Using digital marketing, generate as many leads as possible by selling ideas and solutions. The objective is to draw your target market's attention to your brand. This may be accomplished through SEO, social media marketing, events, and other means. This is the point at which you initially pique a consumer's interest. It may be a tweet, a Facebook post from a friend, a Google search, or something else. Your prospect learns about your company and what you have to offer. When the chemistry is exactly right, customers will occasionally buy straight away. It's a case of being at the right place at the right moment. The consumer has already done their homework and is aware that you provide a desirable product at a reasonable price. More often than not, the awareness stage is more akin to a romance. You're attempting to entice the prospect to return to your website and become more involved with your company.

Step 2: Interest

You want to keep people interested in your brand when they become aware of it. Make your potential consumers interested in learning about the product's benefits and how it is appropriate for them. This phase is all about understanding and honoring the user's wishes. You should avoid being excessively aggressive since this may turn off certain consumers. The goal is to demonstrate your expertise, aid the customer in making an educated selection, and offer to help them in any way you can. At this point, your lead is eager to learn more about you. They may not be ready to buy just yet, but they are considering it. During their downtime, your message should go through their minds. Keep them interested and involved with your story. This is the stage at which you begin to create tales that make your product or service more relevant.

How would your product help them address their problems? Can you fill a void in their life? You must create these stories and consider how you will tell them to people. So, how can you maintain your audience's attention? The importance of consistency cannot be overstated. Create relevant material regularly. This phase of the procedure can be carried out using a variety of tools. Send them an email, interact with them on social media, or drive them to your website. Your leads will always require a reference to look at and consider before making a choice. Customers who reach the sales funnel's interest stage are doing research, comparing pricing, and contemplating their options. This is the opportunity to strike with amazing content that helps them but does not sell to them. You will turn off prospects and drive them away if you push your product or service from the outset. The goal is to demonstrate your expertise, aid the customer in making an educated selection, and offer to help them in any way you can.

Step 3: Decision

Your leads would have evolved into prospects at this stage. They are already familiar with your brand and are curious about what you have to offer. The best part is that they are genuinely willing to make that buy; all they need is a little push! So why not use the iron when it's hot? Provide your prospects with something that will entice them to say yes. How do you go about doing this? Here are several options based on the scenario. When a consumer is ready to buy, they enter the decision stage of the sales funnel. They may be evaluating two or three choices, one of which should be you. This is the moment to make your most competitive offer.

Your consumer is ready to buy and make a decision. They may be evaluating two or three choices, including you. This is the time to make that tempting offer. Offer discounts, package offers, or free delivery. Making the offer more enticing by including exclusive, urgent, and limited-time offerings. It might be free delivery while most of your competitors charge a discount voucher or a free product. In any case, make it so attractive that your prospect can't wait to take advantage of it.

1. **Offer Pricing Offers.** Whether you offer your prospects a realistic pricing page or reductions, their judgments will undoubtedly be influenced. So to provide the greatest offerings, you can entice your prospect and get them to say, "I do."

2. **Provide Testimonials.** Testimonials from previous and current customers influence your prospects' decision-making process. The more authentic testimonials you can provide, the more credibility you will get.
3. **Free Trials.** We want to take something for a test drive before we commit to it. It's the same in marketing and sales. Once your prospect understands the idea of your offering, making a purchase is not difficult.

There are various techniques to get your prospects to purchase your product. For example, you may choose between live demos and experiences. Just make sure that the procedure has a favorable influence on their decisions. When you leave a favorable impression, the sale is almost certain.

Step 4: Action

Finally, we've arrived at the final step! The customer takes action, and your job is to persuade them to do business with you. If the previous three phases were completed, selling should be a breeze. Your consumer will be eager to purchase your goods or services. Once the transaction is completed, your consumer becomes a part of your company's ecosystem. Because your prospect has reached the bottom of the sales funnel, they have become clients. This isn't the end of it. You must ACT to provide them with the greatest possible experience with your product. You must also excite their allegiance to keep them. The client acts at the absolute bottom of the sales funnel.

They buy your product or service and therefore become a part of your company's ecosystem. However, just because a consumer reaches the bottom of the funnel does not imply your job is over. The action is for both the customer and the marketer. You want to do everything you can to turn one purchase into ten, ten into a hundred, and so on. In other words, you're concerned about client retention. Express your appreciation for the purchase, ask your consumer to provide feedback, and make yourself accessible for tech help, if necessary.

1. **Product Tips and Training**. Providing your consumers with product lessons and advice can help them get more familiar with your product. As a result, customers will be able to use your product more effectively and efficiently.
2. **Pricing Package Bundles**. Now that your prospects have become customers, you may continue to make pricing offers more aggressively than before. Offer discounts on their next purchase or packages where they may save even more. Customers are more likely to return when they see things like these.
3. **Campaign and Content Delivery**. Your consumers should be the first to learn about your plans. Maintain consistency in sending them updates and material via email or product messaging. Your promotions and other services may be beneficial to them as well!

Chapter-02: How to build Supersales funnel for consistent sales

Supersales funnel

As previously said, several approaches lead to consumer conversion. However, following the points listed above will help you execute the sales funnel more effectively. The following is a list of elements to consider while developing an efficient sales funnel:

1. Create a business brand and messaging.
2. Engage and connect with your audience.
3. Make sure you provide answers to real-world issues.
4. Increase the effectiveness of your digital marketing tactics.
5. Maintain consistency in all aspects of content distribution, message, and so on.
6. Invest in making profitable proposals.
7. Continuous action equals constant client retention.

In today's fast-paced business environment, creating a good sales funnel must be accurate and current. As a result, you must employ as many approaches as feasible.

Full Scale thinks that finding startup assistance should be simple. It should be quick and inexpensive without sacrificing quality. So that's what we've been doing since the beginning. We assist new firms in creating the product of their dreams to be marketed and sold.

Furthermore, we provide digital marketing services that may help you improve your company's sales funnel tactics.

As a bonus, several firms have utilized their products, such as applications and websites, as sales funnel tools. That being said, you don't need to seek any further software development assistance. That's something we do as well!

Why are a sales funnel important?

The journey prospects follow depicted by your sales funnel. Understanding your funnel might assist you in identifying the funnel's holes - the points at which prospects drop out and never convert.

You can't optimize your sales funnel if you don't understand it. We'll go over how the funnel works in more detail later, but for now, remember that you can affect how visitors travel through the funnel and whether they finally convert.

The Sales Funnel Explained: How it Works

While several terminologies represent distinct sales funnel phases, we'll stick with the four most prevalent to illustrate how each step works as a customer progresses from a visitor to a prospect to a lead to a purchase. First, a visitor arrives at your website via a Google search or a social media link. They are now a candidate. The visitor may read a couple of your blog entries or go through your product listings. At some time, you offer them the opportunity to join your email list. When a visitor completes your form, they become a lead. You may now market to your customers by email, phone, or text – or all three. When you engage leads with special offers, information about new blog articles, or other enticing messaging, they are more likely to return to your website. Perhaps you'll provide a discount code. As visitors progress through the sales funnel, it narrows.

An Effective Sales Funnel Example

Assume you operate an internet store that sells vintage signage. You are aware that your target audience spends a lot of time on Facebook and that your target consumers are males and females between the ages of 25 and 65. You execute an excellent Facebook ad that directs people to a landing page. You ask your prospect to join your email list in return for a lead magnet on the page. Isn't it very straightforward? Instead of prospects, you now have leads. They're making their way through the funnel.

You will send out material over the following several weeks to educate your subscribers about antique signs, offer design ideas, and assist customers in determining how to install these signs. At the end of your email blast, you give each consumer a 10% discount on their whole first order. Bang! You're making a lot of money off of old signage. Everyone wants what you have to offer. Following that, you add the same clients to a new email list. You restart the procedure but with different content. Give them gallery wall ideas, tell them how to care for their signs, and propose signs as presents. You're inviting them to return for more.

You now have it:

1. **Awareness**: You generated a Facebook ad to direct traffic to your website.
2. **Interest**: In exchange for lead acquisition, you provide something of value.
3. **Decision**: Your content educates and prepares your audience to make a purchase.

4. **Action**: You provide an irresistible discount to your leads, then begin marketing to them again to increase retention.

How to Build a Sales Funnel Fast

You're ecstatic now, aren't you? You need to establish a sales funnel right away—and quickly. Don't be concerned. It's not as complicated as it appears.

Step 1: Analyze Your Audience's Behavior

The more you understand your target market, the more effective your sales funnel will be. You aren't marketing to everyone. You're marketing to folks who are a good fit for what you have to offer. Create a Crazy Egg account and begin producing Snapshots. These user behavior reports assist you in monitoring site activity and determining how visitors interact with your site. When do they start scrolling? All of these data pieces will aid in the refinement of your buyer personas.

Step 2: Capture Your Audience's Attention

Your sales funnel will only operate if you can get customers to enter it. This entails exposing your material to your intended audience. Take a natural way and post a lot of material on all of your channels. Diversify your content using infographics, videos, and other forms of media. Run a few advertisements if you're ready to spend more money. The best place to run such advertisements is where your target demographic spends their time. For example, LinkedIn advertising may be the ideal choice if you're selling B2B.

Step 3: Build a Landing Page

Your ad or other material must direct your prospects to a certain location. Therefore, you should ideally send them to a landing page with a can't-miss offer.

Because these customers are still at the bottom of the sales funnel, concentrate on gathering leads rather than pushing the sale.

A landing page's purpose is to move the user to the next step. You need a strong call to action that informs people precisely what they need to do, whether to download a free e-book or watch an instructive video.

Step 4: Create an Email Drip Campaign

By delivering excellent content, you may market to your leads via email. Do so regularly, but not too frequently. One or two emails each week should be plenty.

Build up to the sale by first educating your market. What are they hoping to learn? What roadblocks and objections must you overcome to persuade them to buy?

Make an amazing offer at the end of your drip campaign. That is the kind of knowledge that will compel your prospects to take action.

Step 5: Keep in Touch

Don't forget about your current clients. Instead, keep reaching out to them. Thank them for their purchases, provide extra promo coupons, and invite them to participate in your social media activities.

Chapter-03: Measuring the Success of a Sales Funnel

As your company expands, you learn more about your consumers and diversify your products and services, and your sales may require adjustments. That's OK.

Tracking your conversion rates is an excellent method to gauge the performance of your sales funnel.

For example, how many individuals join up for your email list after clicking on a Facebook ad?

Pay close attention to the following stages of the sales funnel:

- Are you grabbing enough consumers' attention with your initial content?
- Do your prospects have enough faith in you to offer you their contact information?
- Have you received any sales as a result of your email drip campaign and other marketing efforts?
- Do previous clients return to you and buy from you again?

Knowing the explanations will help you decide where your sales funnel needs to be adjusted.

Why Should You Optimize Your Sales Funnel?

Prospective consumers have several alternatives. You'd like people to buy your products or services, but you can't produce them. Instead, you must market effectively. You can only assume what your prospects want if you don't have a tight, efficient sales funnel. If you are incorrect, you will lose the deal. Use Crazy Egg Recordings to see how visitors interact with your site throughout a session. Is there anything that seems to perplex them? Are they paying attention to where you want them to? This is especially crucial for the landing pages we discussed. Most consumers will simply click away if they are not optimized for conversions.

How to Optimize Your Sales Funnel

There are several strategies to enhance your sales funnel. However, the essential regions to concentrate your efforts on are those where customers go to the next funnel stage.

We discussed Facebook Ads. Don't simply run one ad. Run 10 or 20 laps. They may look identical, but route them to separate buyer personas and utilize Facebook's targeting capabilities to ensure they appear in front of your intended audience. Your landing pages should be subjected to A/B testing. It will take time, but you will reach more people and convert more prospects. You may also perform A/B testing on your email campaigns. Alter your wording, graphics, offers, and layouts to see what your target audience responds to. However, paying attention to the outcomes is the greatest approach to enhance your sales funnel. Begin at the top of the funnel. You're generating the content, whether sponsored or organic, to attract people to notice your brand and urge them to click on your call to action. If one piece of material does not work, try another.

Proceed to your landing page. First, make sure the offer and CTA are consistent with the content of your blog post, Facebook ad, or any other asset you used to bring visitors there. To determine what performs best, test your title, body content, pictures, and CTA. Next, a/B test your offer when you invite individuals in the Action step to buy from you. Is free delivery more effective than a 5% discount? These minor adjustments might have a significant impact on your revenue. Finally, keep track of your client retention rate. Do consumers return to you for a second, fifth, or twenty purchase? Do they recommend others? Your objective is to maintain your brand at the forefront of people's minds. If you never let your audience down, they will have no reason to seek elsewhere.

Have you ever wondered how businesses offer their products and services continuously?

When you're selling something, whether it's a cookie, a vehicle, or software, it might be easy to acquire your first sale through friends, peers, or your network. But, in the long run, how can you produce and keep consistent revenue? Consistent sales and profitable enterprises, like anything else, do not happen overnight. A sales funnel the key to achieving consistent sales.

Conversations in groups.

Participating in meaningful online conversations takes time, but it pays off in the long run. Find communities where you know you can contribute value and work to get your name and brand out there by giving support and advice and responding to intriguing postings. Being an active member of your community can benefit you much when you post a link to your free material, website, Facebook page, or products and services.

If you have a free trial of whatever you offer, this might also be a good way to acquire leads. However (and this is a huge but), you must be an active member of groups. Simply putting a link on occasion will not work since there will already be a lot of trust-building going on, and most people will disregard you.

Chapter-04: Building a sales funnel from scratch

A good sales funnel will effortlessly transport someone from top to bottom. But you'll need a method to do so. Don't be concerned. It isn't as complicated as it appears.

KNOW YOUR AUDIENCE

It all starts with identifying your target audience and getting to know them well. Remember this fundamental marketing concept: you are not promoting to everyone. You're promoting to folks who might buy your stuff. Next, determine and analyze your audience's behavior. What piques their interest? What motivates them to press that button? How much time do they spend scrolling across pages? All of these elements will be critical to the success of your sales funnel and subsequent sales and marketing initiatives.

POSTING CONTENT ON ALL YOUR PLATFORMS

Customers must be educated about your products or services. Not only that, but you must continually engage your audience by generating and marketing content across all of your channels. Diversify your content using infographics, videos, and other forms of media.

BUILD A LANDING PAGE

Your content efforts will be in vain if you do not take your prospects someplace. You should ideally direct them to a landing page. The idea here is to concentrate on lead generation rather than closing a transaction.

LAUNCH AN EMAIL CAMPAIGN

Launch a series of emails to drive visitors to your landing pages or website. Create an email campaign that tells a narrative while also addressing your customer's pain points. But be careful not to spam them. Do so regularly, but not too frequently. Finally, finish your excellent emails with a captivating call-to-action that will force your consumers to take action.

CONSISTENTLY REACH OUT

When the consumer makes a purchase, your effort does not end. In reality, you're restarting the funnel phases from the beginning. The experience a consumer has after making their first purchase may either make or ruin your company. The greatest method to remain in touch with them is to provide customer service and request feedback. Additionally, thank them by providing loyalty programs to reward them and deepen your relationship.

WHY ARE A SALES FUNNEL IMPORTANT?

The ideal sales funnel approach does not emerge overnight. Improving insights, rebuilding game plans, and refining targeting all require time. It is difficult labor, but it is critical for your company's survival and success. Your sales funnel will always be the backbone of your company. It may appear to be a lot of labor, but remember that the payoff is well worth it. Don't worry if you've never developed a sales funnel before. The more you practice, the better you will get. Integrate your sales funnel techniques with IgnitePost's existing marketing tools. With our solution, you'll be able to create that sweet spot between digital and personal, which is intended to deliver quick, easy, personalized handwritten notes from your existing marketing or CRM systems.

Successful Sales Funnels Need Filling Constantly

In reality, a sales funnel is a very basic notion. You start at the top and work your way down, bringing your leads and prospects closer to the prize of purchasing your product or service. Effectively nurturing that sales funnel is the hallmark of a successful firm, and technology like Sales Radar helps ensure you're doing so. But you can't grow something out of anything. You can't develop relationships if you don't know who you're talking to. So, as we're sure you've heard, you need to keep filling the funnel from the top. But what precisely does it include, and how do you do it? There are some really simple techniques that successful businesses utilize to fill their funnels. Here are some of our favorites and some general tips to make them all work better.

Here are five tried-and-true methods for consistently filling your sales funnel

Talking to strangers

One of the most apparent methods to attract individuals to the top of your funnel is business networking. There are several events and organizations where you may meet other company owners who require what you sell. Search for local networking events and attend a few before determining which one(s) will work best for your personality and business. But, like with any marketing, there are incorrect and good methods to accomplish it.

Network; don't sell

Make an effort to converse with strangers and show an interest in them. Begin an engaging discussion and learn to recognize the signals that may require what you have to give. Approaching networking with a sales mindset may backfire spectacularly. No one wants to talk to someone who appears desperate and solely interested in selling. Instead, chat to individuals just to talk to them, and perhaps add them to your email list if you're excellent at providing important or entertaining information that will assist them. You don't want to look spammy, so make sure you acquire permission beforehand.

Work on your elevator pitch.

Many networking events will provide you the opportunity to explain to the individuals in the room what you do. Even if you don't have this opportunity, it's a good idea to write the perfect description of what you do in a few lines. A good rule of thumb here is to convey the value you offer with your product or service in 140 characters or less in a tweet or SMS. This is also called the elevator pitch since it should be brief enough to explain in less than a minute. Keep things simple, and you'll be remembered more.

Speak up

If you are allowed to speak at an event, take advantage of it. Being the keynote speaker at any event is a wonderful method to generate leads since you will have the most effect on the event than anyone else. Give some good value and assist the audience with a few pointers on what you do. If you demonstrate your knowledge, you will get trust, which is what networking is all about.

Follow up

One of the primary reasons you won't be effective at networking is that you view the discussions you have at meetings as the conclusion of the conversation rather than the beginning. If you believe you might help each other further, attempt to follow up with an email, phone, or even a coffee after every interaction you have during a networking gathering. Even if that individual does not require your services right now, they may suggest you to your next customer or require you in the future.

Be useful

It is all too simple to attend a networking event only to further your business. A great networker will see it as an opportunity to be a community member and serve that community by connecting individuals. A person who effectively links people in their network to others will receive significantly more for their business based only on the rule of reciprocity. Others will just want to compensate you for your referrals. It's excellent karma for business!

Be an exhibitionist!

An expo or business show is an excellent method to collect many business cards, leads, and contacts all at once. Having an eye-catching stand and having several short discussions about your business is a tried and true method of getting your organization, product, or service out there.

Chapter-05: Successful lead generation at an exhibition

Stand out and stand up!

It goes without saying that if you're going to exhibit at a show, you'll have to go above and beyond if you want it to be a success. There will be a lot of other businesses at the expo, so you'll have to compete for attention right away. Get your stand designed to attract the proper individuals, and include something on it that draws them in rather than drives them away. We hired a magician to perform card tricks with business cards at a recent presentation to demonstrate our business card scanning software. Not only did we have a long line, but we also collected a lot of business cards, which turned into new leads for our funnel. Oh, and get rid of the chairs. Nothing says "I can't be bothered to chat to you," like uninterested folks sitting on chairs gazing at their phones. Sorry, but you might want to invest in some comfortable shoes for the day.

Follow up (again)

Yes, we've returned to the task of following up. Exhibiting, like networking, will need following up on and continuing all of those discussions. You may have some specific warm leads to pursue, or you may simply want to get to know them. Treat each type of discussion differently, and have a structure to keep things simple yet quick. Following up after a concert should be done as soon as possible so that you remain fresh in their minds.

Attractive content

Creating useful material such as blogs, vlogs, videos, and eBooks is still an excellent method to get new leads and contacts. You may produce material to give away in return for email addresses and then cultivate relationships with those leads by email, mail, or even more items. Don't go for the hard sale, just like you wouldn't with any other relationship-building technique. Instead, send out good material, followed by useful emails, and slowly upsell them to larger and better items as needed.

Facebook Ads

Facebook ads are by far the most cost-effective and efficient approach to get your content in front of relevant connections. Consider your ideal prospect (also known as a customer persona) and produce content, advertisements, and targeted audiences for them. You must develop content and advertisements that are unmissable and ideal for your prospects as they scroll through Facebook. Consider what 'pain' they are experiencing and how you might assist them, and then begin from there.

Website lead magnets

You'll undoubtedly receive visitors to your website, so don't allow them to go without providing you an opportunity to assist them. Creating a free download or eBook for your website may be a great way to collect visitors' email addresses. However, as with any marketing, you must consider what occurs after they receive your fantastic download. According to research, not everyone will read it; therefore, the follow-up is more important than the material they receive first.

Socially acceptable

Social media is a powerful source of the traffic to a website, brand, or business - but it can also be a leaky funnel if you're not cautious. Social media discussions are a strong indicator of interest – especially during a business event – but it's easy to lose track of all of them.

Get them on your list

Your email list might be the next step in your social media funnel. Gaining followers and admirers are fantastic, but email addresses are even more vital for a business. It is doubtful that Facebook will cease operations tomorrow, but who knows what may occur in the future. You will always own their emails (until they unsubscribe); therefore, it is worthwhile to have them on your list if possible.

Build Twitter lists

At the very least, if you compile all of your prospects into a Twitter list, you'll have them all in one spot. This is an excellent strategy for approaching a concert, lecture, or event. Anyone you speak with should be added to a list. At an expo, an easy method to accomplish this is to have a selfie or customized hashtag competition on your booth, and then after the event, go back to your hashtag and add them from there.

Conclusion

Building a sales funnel from the ground up for a startup necessitates the recruiting and training a sales staff. It will take time and money for them to reach peak production. Outsourcing some operations inside a sales funnel might be one approach to cut expenses and acquire experience. Businesses outsource lead generation services to save money on employing an internal staff and paying for pricey software in many situations. Sales are frequently performed by the founder/owner of a startup. They could have a network of potential customers. However, after their network has run dry, they will need to create a powerful sales funnel. The establishment of a high-performing sales staff is required for the company's success. Here's where things may go wrong: Not many CEOs have prior sales expertise. They frequently lack knowledge in developing a sales funnel, a sales process, and processes, particularly when it comes to lead generation, which is still relatively new to many individuals. The unfortunate reality of a sales funnel is that it leaks at every stage. You will not get everyone who enters your funnel to buy from you at the bottom, no matter how hard you try. Many of them will abandon your sales funnel at various times. This is why you must constantly adding new leads to it and why you should nurture rather than assault your funnel. Set up a strong strategy for following up, engaging, and determining when it's time to go for the sale. Not everyone will move at the same rate, and not everyone will purchase - that is simply how business works. Using a system like Sales Radar can help you make the most of all your leads and ensure you don't miss any chances... but it's up to you to keep it up to date!

www.ingramcontent.com/pod-product-compliance
Lightning Source LLC
Chambersburg PA
CBHW030040230526
45472CB00002B/595